# WORKBOOK for

## THE REST OF THE GOSPEL: When the Partial Gospel Has Worn You Out
## by Dan Stone and Greg Smith

## Barbara Moon

My thanks go to Greg Smith for putting Dan's words into book form and giving me permission to write the guide and workbook.

## To The Student

You will need a copy of *The Rest of the Gospel: When the Partial Gospel Has Worn You Out*. This workbook can be used for homework or note taking in a group, or it can be used for personal study alone. The book's page numbers from which a question is taken are in parentheses after each question, with the "answers" at the end of the workbook. Some of the questions are personal. For use in a group there is a Leader's Guide.

The theme of *The Rest of the Gospel* is the Christian's union with Christ and freedom from living by self-effort. Dan's focus is to view life from God's perspective and not man's, to be Christ centered instead of self-centered, and to answer the question all Christians long to know, "Where's the Life?" Dan and Greg back their points with Scripture and practical application.

Many Christians struggle with what to do with difficult circumstances, how to view problems in life and how to walk in victory. All know that their sins are forgiven—the first half of the Gospel. *The Rest of the Gospel* will help you to understand how God views you through what His Son has done on the Cross and will give you truths that bring victory and freedom to your walk with Christ—the second half of the Gospel.

Take your time through this study. It is not one to be taken lightly and then set aside. It is the very foundation of our Christian life. It is a study that bears periodic repeating throughout our life, until we are as certain that we are one with Christ as we are that our sins are forgiven, until the Holy Spirit teaches us our union with Christ both by "revelation and experience."

Barbara Moon

# Table of Contents

# WORKBOOK FOR

## *The Rest of the Gospel* by Dan Stone & Greg Smith

**By Barbara Moon**

### PREFACE

1. Have you ever thought about the fact that God might receive glory through you? What might that mean?


2. What happens if we do not look at the Christian life from God's point of view? What are some characteristics of being man-centered? (p. 1)


3. How has God blessed us? (p.2)


4. What purpose did God have for us before the foundation of the world?


5. Why do we exist? (p. 3)

6. What is our part in God's plan?

7. Look at the verse on page 12 (last page of Preface) and talk about why the three words are italicized.


8. Where can we find everything we need to know for experiencing God's abundant life?


9. Why does Christ live in us?

## CHAPTER ONE—THE GATES

1.  What do you think Dan means by his statement, "Where's the life?" What do you think this life would look like? (pp. 15-16)

2.  What does Dan say about the first Gate we go through as a Christian? What does he mean by "externals?" What funny item does he compare this first gate to? (p. 17)

3. What are some of the externals you have added to your wardrobe to give you a new external identity?

4. What is the main thing that a person knows by revelation in this first gate? (p. 18)

5. What has to happen before we can go through the second gate? (p. 19)

6. What is the second gate? (p.20) What was/is your second gate like?

7. Upon what is this second gate based? (p. 21) What about yours?

8.  What did Dan learn that helped him at this stage? (p. 22)

9. What had to happen before he could go through the third gate?

10. What is the third gate? (p. 22)

11. How did Dan come to understand the third gate? What are some of the concepts? (p. 23)

12. What was one of Barbara Stone's externals and how did God deal with it? (p. 24)

13. What does Dan call the circumstances that God uses to bring us to the end of ourselves as the point of reference? (p. 25)


## CHAPTER TWO—THE LINE

1. What is Dan's teaching tool based on 2 Cor. 4:18?  What are the two truths it contains? (Pp. 27-28)


2. Give some specific characteristics of both of these realms?  Come up with some ideas that are not in the book so that you will really understand the differences. (p. 28-29)


3. Where should our focus be? (p. 29)


4. Why does it matter that Jesus came below the line and is above the line also? (p. 29)


5. What are some things that are already true of us?  (p. 30)


6.  What are the three reasons that it is vital to distinguish between the two realms? (p. 30-31)


7. Give some characteristics of each of these reasons. (pp. 30-31)


8. What important things are based in the unseen and eternal realm?  (p. 32)  What makes this difficult?

9. What determines the degree to which we live in this realm? (p. 32)

10.  How do we get an inner knowing?  (p. 32)

11. What is it that always determines how we live? (p. 33) Discuss how this works.

12. What happens if we do not know that sin no longer has power over us? (p. 33)

13. What will we live by if we do not know the unseen and eternal is home to us?

14. What is the most important thing we can know from this realm? (p. 33)

15. On page 34 talk about some of the characteristics of a life that knows union.

16. Look at each verse that ends the chapter.  How do we operate these truths? What do they say about us? Which part of us are they talking about? Is it difficult for you to accept that these are true of you?

## CHAPTER THREE—DOUBLE CROSS, PART ONE

1. What were the only two messages Dan knew to give before knowing union?  (p. 35)

2. What is the first side of the cross?  (p. 36)

3. Do you know without any doubt that your sins are forgiven?

4. What are some questions we often ask when only knowing our sins are forgiven? (p. 37)

5. How do we take the revelation that our sins are forgiven and try to stretch it over to cover how to live the life? (p. 37)

6. Where does this kind of activity put our focus? (p. 38) How are we seeing ourselves?


7. What is the outcome of living from the flesh/independent self-effort? (p. 38)


8. What is the difference in "sins" and "sin?" (p. 39)


9. What can a person's life look like if they do not know that the "sin" issue has been taken care of? (p.39)

10. How do most people think the problem will be taken care of? (p. 39)


11. When does God intend for us to experience victory over sin/sins? (p. 39)


12. What did Dan conclude was the real issue or question? (p. 40)


13. How did understanding Romans 6:3-6 change Dan's life?




14. What does the word "baptize" mean? What difference does that make to your Christian walk? (p. 40-41)




*[On the next page is my personal rendition of Dr. Charles Solomon's line diagram. It can be found in his book, Handbook to Happiness on page 40. Studying this diagram can be very helpful. I emphasize that being in Adam or in Christ means "Whatever happened to Adam, happened to me, Whatever is true of Adam is true of me; then Whatever happened to Christ happened to me, Whatever is true of Christ is true of me. ]*

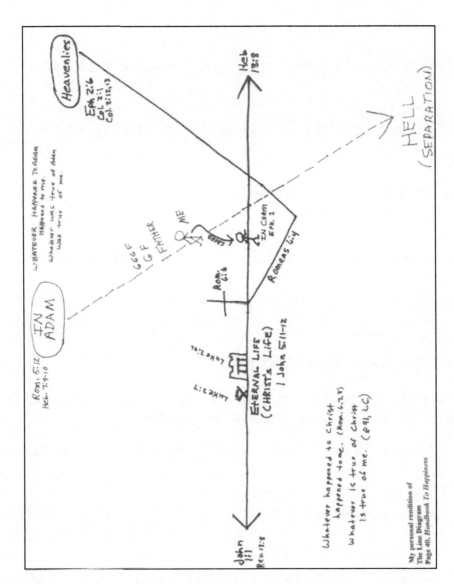

**Diagram 1.** My rendition of Dr. Charles Solomon's Line Diagram from *Handbook to Happiness*

15. What actually died with Christ? How does Dan describe this? (p. 41)

16. What is the "old man?" With what did God replace the old man? (p. 42)

17. Look at the verb tenses on page 42 that Dan italicizes. This paragraph contains parts of verses in Ephesians 2:1-3. Read that passage all the way to verse 6. What difference does it make to know the tenses of these verbs? (In the future as you read books such as Ephesians, Colossians, Romans, begin to notice the verb tenses.)

18. What is the first side of the cross?  What are its characteristics? (p. 42)


19.  What is the second side of the cross and its characteristics? (p. 42-43)


20. How does communion relate to the two sides of the cross?  (p. 43)


21. Why does it matter to know the second side that most people don't know?



## CHAPTER FOUR—WHAT YOU DIED TO

*Review-- sin and sins from page 39.  Review what baptize means; the analogy of the dandelion; emphasize the two sides—sins forgiven, we died.*

1. Why do you think the 80 year old lady was so excited to know she had died? (p. 45-46)


2.  What are some aspects of the "old man?" (p. 46)


3.  Look at the verses on Page 46.  Though Christ died for all, what do we as individuals have to do to experience this?


4.  Look at Hebrews 7:9-10.  How does this story relate to us dying in Christ?  (p. 47)


5. What does Dan say most people think about "all?"  (p. 47)


6. What do we do to ourselves when we don't really know that we died with Christ? (p. 47)


7.  What does the word "reckon" (that Dan mentions on page 47) mean in the KJV of Romans 6:11?

8. Look at 2 Corinthians 5:17-18. How is a creation different from a product? From what does one make a creation? How does this make a difference in how we can look at and accept ourselves? (p. 47)

9. How does Dan explain the terms position and condition that some teachers use? (p. 48)

10. In the third paragraph on page 48, Dan talks about what we can know after God reveals these truths to us. How do we get that revelation to happen?

11. What was the first thing we died **to** when we died with Christ? (p. 48)

12. What is going on when a person hears that grace is license to sin? (p. 48)

13. On page 49 where Dan says that a Christian can do whatever he wants to, what does this really mean?

14. Then why does a Christian sin? (p. 49)

15. On page 50, what does Dan say was not our problem before receiving Christ? What was our problem? How did Christ solve this problem?

16. Where did this problem reside? (p. 50)

17. Why can we still be tempted to sin? (p. 50)

18. What happens when we live by soul thoughts and feelings and by appearances? (p. 50)

19. How will the truth of who we are in Christ show up externally? (p. 51)

20. What is the second thing we died **to**? (p. 51)

21. Look at Romans 7: 1-4. What is the analogy of the husband dying for the wife to be free?  Look at verse 4 and see who it was that died? Who is the husband?


22. Why did God crucify us to the law? (p. 52 two places)


23. How does the law hinder God's purpose in our lives? (p. 52) Look also at Romans 8:1-4


24. What is our certain outcome if we try to keep the law? (p. 52)


25. What is the third thing we died **to**? (p. 53)


26. Why is it impossible for a person to know their union and live out of it if they don't know they died with Christ? (p. 53)


27.  What are the three things we died **to**? (p. 54)


28. How can a person keep from knowing their union?    What might help one to learn it? (p. 54)


## CHAPTER FIVE—DOUBLE CROSS, PART TWO

1. What did Dan learn from 1 John 4: 15? Compare this verse to John 14:20.  (p. 55)


2. What did God purpose to be resurrected from our death with Christ?  (p. 56)

3. What is one of the reasons that God raised our new man from the dead? (p. 56)

4. How did the Passover foreshadow both sides of Christ's work on the cross? (p. 57)

5. What is significant about the Israelites eating the lamb? (p. 57-58)

6. What happens if we try to generate the life?  How do we get the life? (p. 58)

7. What are two ways we are saved?  (p. 58-59)

8. What is the definition of "eternal life?"  (p. 59)

9. What does Dan say often offends people?  Do you know that Christ lives as you? (p. 59)

10. What is the opposite of life? How can our results look like life and not be? How do we know the difference?  (p. 59-60)

11. What does the life of God living through us look like?  Who lives this life? (p. 60-61)

12. Does a Christian want to sin?  (p. 61)

13.  What are the three questions that Dan boils life down to? (p. 62)

14. What is our part in getting the revelation on these truths?  (p. 62)

15. Look at 1 Corinthians 6:17, 2 Corinthians 4:7 and 2 Corinthians 3:16.  What are these verses saying to you?

## CHAPTER SIX—THE SWING

1. What circumstance did God use to teach Dan the difference in his soul and spirit? (p. 65-66)

2. Look at 2 Corinthians 4:18.  How and which part of this verse did God use to speak to Dan?  (p. 67) Study the diagram below of the heart that illustrates this verse. What does it say to you about your feelings and pulls towards the externals?

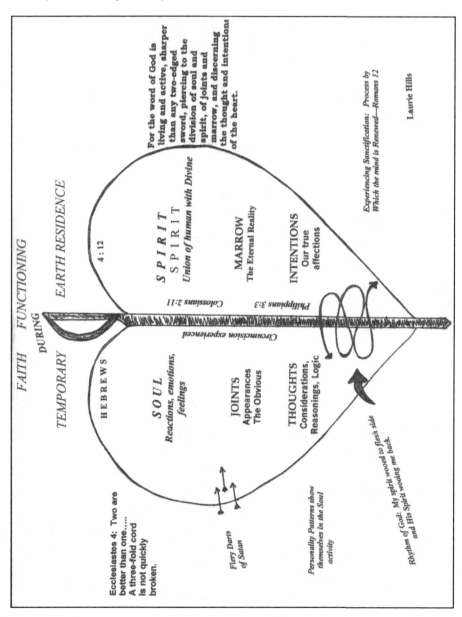

**Diagram 2.**   Hebrews 4:12 by Laurie Hill's. Used with permission from *Jewels for My Journey* by Barbara Moon

3. Why do we usually confuse our soul and spirit? (p. 67)

4. Earlier Dan showed us three things we had to know we died to. What is the second revelation we have to have? (p. 68)

5. How will Satan use things against us if we don't know this second revelation? (p. 68)

6. Discuss how the analogy of a hurricane relates to the soul and spirit. (p. 69)

7. Go over the components of Dan's swing illustration. What does this say to you about your daily life? (p. 70)

8. What is the purpose of a swing?  Why do we not like our swing to swing?  What do we try to do with our swinging? (p. 70-71)

9. Why do we try to nail our swing up on "God's side?"  Why is that not okay? (p. 71)

10. Look at Genesis 2:17 and Genesis 3: 1-5.  What can we learn about our interpretation of good and bad?  What does Dan mean by all that is good is not God? (p. 71)

11. What is the problem with focusing on our soul? (p. 72)

12. Why will you never get your swing to stop swinging?

13. Why did God make our swing to swing? (p. 72)

14. What is wrong with the expression "crucify the self?" (p. 72)

15. What are some results when we realize the swing is not a problem? (p. 72-73)

16. How does our view of God change when we live out of our spirit? (p. 73)

17. What is one of the main differences in the soul and spirit and how are we meant to live with those differences? (p. 73)

18. How does our spirit know something? How does it not know? (p. 74)

19. Discuss the story of Elijah and how it applies to the soul and spirit. (p. 74-75)

20. What determines which place you live according to? (p. 76)

21. In Elijah's story, how is "God in it but not in it?" (p. 76)

22. What does God do with our messes or the devil's messes? (p. 76. See Hebrews 12:11)

23. How does God speak to us? (p. 76-77, see 2 Corinthians 10:5)

24. As you are asking God to show you the difference in the soul and spirit, what is your stand until then?

## CHAPTER SEVEN—ONE SPIRIT

1. What is the only way we can understand a mystery? (p. 79)

2. What are the mysteries Dan talks about on page 81?

3. How does the union work? (p. 81)

4. How will we more fully manifest the life of God? (p. 81)

5. Why do we not have to try to get closer to God? (p. 81)

6.  What are some "old tapes" about yourself and God that go through your mind that are really from believing separation and not union?

7. What is the Tree of Life? (p. 82)

8. How does Jesus look when living through us?  (p. 82)

9.  Discuss Dan's illness and what God showed him through it. (p. 82)

10. How do you know God's voice? What are you doing to learn His voice?

11. What kinds of statements was Dan making in his conversation with God? (p. 83)

12. As Dan discusses the below the line example of union what does he say is the male's role?  The female's role?  (p. 83)

13. Whose life is the wife expressing when she is pregnant?

14. If we try to produce life on our own, what does God call that? (p. 84 See Isaiah 64:6)

15. What does the Bible mean by "flesh" and how is that different than the old man or old nature?

14. How can Dan say that all we humans are "females?"  (p. 84)

15. How do we live as Jesus did according to page 85?

16. Can a pregnant woman keep from manifesting the life in her?  What will happen with the baby? (p. 85)

17. How does knowing this, that the baby will come forth, affect you and your faith journey?

18. What is our part in the process of our faith journey?

## CHAPTER EIGHT—ONE NATURE

1.  What is the rut that most Christians fall into and drive in?  (p. 89)

2. Why does it matter that we believe this rut or not?

3. What is the way out of this dilemma? (p. 90)

4. Why does it matter which realm is reality to us?  (p. 90)

5. Is it easy to believe that we are not both good and evil?  What do we have to stop focusing on in order to not believe it?

6. There are many "either – ors" in the Scripture. Go through the rest of the Chapter and list all the "twos" that Dan gives. Then go back and look at each one.  (pp. 91-95)


7.  What are the two trees?  What happened when we ate of the wrong tree? (p. 91) [Remind of Dr. Solomon's line diagram]


8. What are two masters? (p. 92)


9. What would people decide if looking at Dan and his friend's behavior? What was the truth? (p. 92)


10. What are the two fathers? (p. 93)


11. Why were the Pharisees saying that Jesus was of the devil? (p. 93)


12. What determines who we are in the eternal realm? (p. 93)


13. Who are the two Adams?  (p. 93)


14. Why is it easy to believe we have two natures? (p. 94)


15. What are the two types of slaves?  (p. 94)


16. When we think it is natural for us to sin as a Christian, how do we view God?  (p. 94)


17.  Who are the two husbands in Romans 7: 1-6? (p. 94)

18. What happens if we try to go back to the old husband?  What if we try to produce offspring? (p. 95)


19. What are the two vessels?  (p. 95)


20. What are the two spirits? (p. 95)


21. What is a question we can ask ourselves when doubting our identity? (p. 95)


22. What are the two things we can **do**?   Does this mean that we can **be** both? (p. 96)


23. Why does the teaching on two natures seem so persuasive? (p. 96) To what are we supposed to look to determine who we are?


24. Look at Dan's illustration about Mrs. Jones and Mrs. Baker. What does this illustration say to you about behavior determining who you are? (p. 96)


25.  What is the result of believing that we have two natures?  Who is doing all the work to look good? (p. 96)


26. What determines our identity?  What does not determine it?  (p. 97)

## CHAPTER NINE—THE REAL YOU

1. What are some ways that we get programmed to believe that actions/behavior determine our worth and identity? (p. 99-100)

2. What does Dan's description of marriage say to you? (p. 100)

3. What is part of Satan's plan? (p. 100)

4. What is the false self and what are some of its characteristics? (p. 100)

5. Discuss some examples of how flesh can produce things that look good on the outside. (p. 100)

6. After getting saved and our sins forgiven, what do we usually fall back on? What are some characteristics of this kind of life? (p. 101) Where does the damage we received growing up come in to play? What are some of your "flesh patterns?"

7. Until we stop seeing our humanity as all important, what is our focus? (p. 101)

8. What are some ways that you go by performance and appearances?

9. What does 2 Corinthians 5:14-16 tell us about how to look at Christ, others and ourselves? (p. 101)

10. Look at 2 Corinthians 5: 17-18, Ezekiel 36:26, John 3: 6-8, Ephesians 2:6 and Ephesians 4:24). Notice the verb tenses. What do these verses say about you? (p. 102)

11. What is the definition of "creation?" How does that differ from a "product?"

12. Why does it matter whether or not we believe these truths about ourselves?

13. What is the importance of saying God's truth *after* the "but?" (p. 102)

14. Do you believe that God keeps score? (p. 102)

15. When did Dan come to the end of trying to make himself new? (p. 103)

16. How does God look at you and what does He see?   (p. 103, 104) Make a list of all that God says about you. Whisper to God, "I am holy and righteous, I am _____," (each of the attributes.) Say to Him, "You delight in me." You might see how hard it can be to take these truths. Put the attributes from this page onto a card and put it on your mirror.

17. What does "complete" mean?  (p. 104) Discuss the differences between being mature in the unseen and eternal and the seen and temporal.  What are some different kinds of maturity? What is our part in growing maturity below the line?  How does this work?

18. What is the first benefit of knowing our true identity that Dan talks about on page 104?

19. How can we know the difference in God's voice and Satan's voice? (p. 104) Make a list of some of the attributes that are opposites.

20. What is the second benefit of knowing our true identity on page 105

21. How do we know if we have sinned or not? (p. 105)

22.  What do we do when the Holy Spirit makes it clear that we have sinned?  (p. 106) (Look at 1 John 1:9. Confess means agree with.)

23. What does Dan say about calling ourselves sinners?

24. After we have agreed with God about a sin, rather than ask forgiveness, what would be better? (p. 106)

25. What does it mean to live out of our flesh? (p. 106) What kind of life is it? What does it look like?

26. What is an idol? (p. 107) Name some ways you might be feeding your identity. When would it be alright to have these externals?

27. What is the answer to the false self? (p. 107)

28. Where does getting help from counseling and healing come in to our journey? (p. 108)

29. Who are you at the deepest level of your personhood? (p. 108)

30. What is your part in appropriating these truths? (p. 108, 109)

## CHAPTER TEN—GOD'S PRECIOUS ASSETS

1.  What is the definition of an asset?

**Diagram 3**. Because of what Christ has done on the Cross, when we receive Him as our life, we are as valuable as He.

2. What is the definition of a liability?  (p. 111)

3. What will be the results of living under the false idea that we are a liability to God? (p.111)

4. What about even if we are "messing up?" (p. 111)

5. Why does our humanity have to be part of God's plan? (p. 112)

6. How does the way a radio works compare to us being God's assets? (p. 112)

7. Which parts of us as humans does God need to express Himself? Are there any parts of yourself that you are rejecting and not seeing as God sees? (p. 112-113)

8. Discuss the difference in being a container/vessel versus being the contents. (p. 113, 2 Cor. 4:7)

9. What will a life look like that does not know that God is the life in the vessel?

10. What are some of the characteristics of a mirror? How does this apply to us and God? Are you able to look in the mirror and see Jesus? (p. 114)

11. What are two aspects of being an earthen vessel? (p. 114)

12. What does it look like if we are trying to be someone who we are not? (p. 114)

13. What is true rest all about? (p. 114, Hebrews 4: 9-11, Matthew 11:29)

14. What happened to our personality at salvation?  How does sanctification fit in with union?  Which part of us does God change after salvation?  (p. 115)

15. What makes it easier for people to relate to us and listen to things we are trying to tell them? (p. 115)

16. What can we do to accept the things that we do not like until and if God changes them? (p. 116, Philippians 2:3, Phil. 1:6)

17.  What about traits or habits which are harmful to ourselves or others?

18. Look at Dan's example about being a lemon on page 116. What are some of your "warts and imperfections" that you can or need to accept and leave to God?

19. Where does variety fit into us being God's assets?  (p. 117, Ephesians 4:11, Galatians 5: 1, 1 John 4:7-9)

20. How did Dan come to be satisfied with being himself?  (p. 118)

## CHAPTER ELEVEN—REVELATION:  GOD'S WAY OF KNOWING

1.  What is the difference in intellectual understanding and spiritual understanding? (p. 121, 122)

2. How does the frustration of *knowing about* and wanting to do better before we have the revelation of *knowing* work to our advantage?  How does God view our efforts?  (p. 122)

3. How do our battles in the visible realm fit with God's plan of teaching us to live in the invisible? (p. 123)

4. What are some examples of "flesh questions?" "Flesh answers?" (p. 123)


5. What are some examples of "spirit questions?" "Spirit answers?" (p. 123) [6. How do we finally get spirit answers? (p. 123)



7.  Who is the answer?  (p. 123)

8. How does the Spirit give us the answers?  (p. 124)


9. What is the difference in "know about" and "know?" (p. 125) [Compare with above on p. 123]


10. When we live from "know about" how do we live? (p. 125)


11. What happens when the Spirit of God changes your mind or shows you truth?  (p. 125)


12.  Do you know beyond a doubt that your sins are forgiven? What else does God want you to <u>know</u> as deeply as you know your sins are forgiven? (p. 126)


13. What is "knowing" <u>not</u>?  (p. 126)  Why is it important not to rely on these instead of on truly knowing?



14. What are the two ways that the Holy Spirit teaches us?  Describe them. (p. 126)



15. What does God use to work the experience into our walk? (p. 126)

16 How does "Adam knew his wife" correlate to us knowing God's truths? (p. 126)  Give some examples of things that are mixed together and become one.

17. How do we learn algebra or carpentry or engineering or sales, etc.?

18. What happens after an "Oh, I see?"  (p. 127) Where does this take place?

19. How does God teach us?  What does He use?   Who decides when it will happen? (p. 128)

20. Whom does the Holy Spirit glorify?  What is His role in the trinity?  (p. 129)

21.  What is our part in cooperating with God in this process? (p. 129)

22. What three things did Dan finally agree to believe that he did not feel were true? (p. 129, 130)

23. What do we always live out of in the end?  (p. 130)

24. How and what does the Spirit use to work our revelations into our experience?  (p. 130)

## CHAPTER TWELVE—THE SINGLE EYE

1. What circumstance did God use to teach Dan about source and security? (p. 131, 132) What is your security?

2. What choice did Dan make to walk through that circumstance with God? (p. 132)

3. Why is it important to see everything in our life as having a God reason? (p. 132)

4. How does God get our attention in a specific area? (p. 132)

5. What does the Bible call this—seeing through our circumstances to God? (p. 133)

6. What does seeing with the Single Eye mean to your daily life and how does Dan's line fit with it?

7. What does Dan do with the argument about who causes things, God or Satan? (p. 134)

8. How do many people decide if God is working or not? (p. 135)

9. How can we say that the negatives, trials, tribulations, etc. are God working? (p. 135, 136)

10. Why does God want us to stay here in the seen and temporal realm? (p. 136)

11. How does Dan show that he is not saying God is the author of evil? (p. 136, 137)

12. What does the Single Eye help us do with our "sacrificial lambs" and hard circumstances? (p. 137) Who has been one of your sacrificial lambs?

13. How did Dan knowing the soul and spirit help him grieve for his wife Barbara? (p. 138)

14. What does God do with our "dry periods?" (p. 138) How has God used one of your dry periods?

15. How can we encourage one another in a present dry period? (p. 138)

16. Ultimately, for whom are our difficult times and lessons? (p. 138, 139, 2 Corinthians 1: 3-7)

## CHAPTER THIRTEEN—THE RULE OF GRACE

*[I like to begin by reading the whole book of Galatians aloud to the group, at least through Chapter 5, substituting the word "behavior" or "performance" any place the word "law" is used.]*

1. What generally makes living the Christian life so difficult and why? (p. 141-142)

2. What was Paul's message to the Galatians after their salvation? (p. 142)

3. Who were the Judaizers and what were they telling the Galatians? (p. 142)

4. Look at Galatians 2: 11-15. Discuss what happened between Paul and Peter and what Paul told Peter, (Galatians 2: 15:16). (p. 143)

5. Can law and grace flow together like two rivers?  Why or why not? (Galatians 3: 1-3, Galatians 4:7)   (p. 144)

6. What happens if we can keep some of the laws but can't keep them all, all the time? (Galatians 5: 3) (p. 144)

7. What in us thinks we can keep the law? (p. 144)

8. Is the law bad?  (See Romans 7: 12, Galatians 3:23-26)

9. What will trying to live by the law bring to us?  (p. 144, 145) Is there anywhere in your life that you are still trying to keep the law by trying to be okay by performing?

10. What is the purpose of failure? (p. 145)

11. If you fail are you a failure?

12. What does Galatians 2:20 have to do with the law and what is it telling us? (Galatians 3:2) (p. 145)

13. With whom was the Abrahamic covenant made?  Why is this important concerning the law? (p. 146)

14. Why does Paul say, "No Way," to having Moses *and* Jesus together in our walk? (Galatians 2:21, 3:21)(p. 146)

15. What is the result of marrying law and grace? (p. 147)

16. Why can it be lonely to walk free from the law?  (p. 147)

17. Why do we need to *know* that we died to the law? (p. 147)


18. Do you find yourself putting too much emphasis on the Bible and not enough on the Spirit? How can you find that balance?


19. What can we tell someone who wants to live under the law? (p. 148)


20. What does Dan say on page 148 about law and grace not flowing together?


21. Why would Dan say to thank God for the time we spent trying to keep the law? (p. 148, Colossians 2:6)


22. What does Paul say about how to keep from walking in the flesh or under the law? (Galatians 5: 16) *[Explain to the group that most churches/Christians walk or believe like this verse is reversed in its order, resulting in living under the law and self effort.]*


23. What are some other words for "law" or "living by the law?" *[Behavior, self-effort, performance, co-dependency, non-acceptance, not seeing things or people through God's eyes. Sometimes I tell people to read the book of Galatians and substitute "behavior" or "performance" or even "co-dependency" everywhere they see the word law.]*


## CHAPTER FOURTEEN—WHO DOES WHAT?

1. What is Dan saying about the rope climbing and our efforts to fix ourselves and others? (p. 152)


2. How is the Christian life totally grace? (p. 152)


3. What happens when we do not know that it is totally grace? (p. 152)


© 2009 Barbara Moon

4. How are we to view the verses about being holy without trying to be holy becoming works? (p. 152)

5. Look at Ezekiel 36:26-27 and discuss all the *I will's* in the passage. What does each mean and represent? (p. 152, 153)

6. How are we to look at keeping the law? What does it mean that we have died to the law? (p. 153, Romans 8:4)

7. What does Dan mean by "point of origin?" (p. 153)

8 . Look at Jeremiah 31:31-34 and list the *I will's* in this passage. Compare them with the ones from Ezekiel. What do they mean in your daily life?

9. Do you understand and believe that the desire of your heart is to walk in the Lord's statues? (p. 153)

10. When we do not believe that this is true, what do we try to do? (p. 154)

11. Make a list of and discuss the *I wills* that are completed in the spirit realm. (p. 154)

12. Which things are ongoing and how does that work? (p. 154)

13. What is our part in the process? (p. 154)

14. What lie did Adam and Eve believe in the Garden?  What does this mean?  What are the results if one is successful?  If one fails?  (p. 155)

15. What are some circumstances and life lessons that God has used to show you that you cannot live the life on your own?

16. What is Christ's purpose in us now?  What is the Holy Spirit's role in us?  (p. 155)

17. Why is ongoing revelation needed?  How does this affect our behavior?  (p. 155)

18. Look at 2 Corinthians 3:18.  What does from "glory to glory" mean? (p. 155)

19. Describe the characteristics of a soulical man.  (p. 156, 1 Corinthians 3:1)

20. Why do "babes in Christ" need dos and don'ts for a while?  (p. 156-157)

21. What does Colossians tell us was Paul's goal for his converts rather than giving them specific dos and don'ts? (p. 157-158)

22. When does a Christian need less of the milk of dos and don'ts?  How does that affect our bent to sin? (p. 158)

23. When we understand our union and that Christ will do the living through us, how will that affect our striving? (p. 158)

24. Why do people use religious activity when they do not understand grace? (p. 159)


25. Why can a Christian stop trying to crucify self? (p. 159)


26. What again is our part in the process of growth and how does it operate? (p. 159)


27. Where does obedience come in to this process and walk in union?  (p. 159, Romans 1:5)

28. What is the work of faith? (p. 159-160, Hebrews 4:11)


29. What does the word "reckon" mean (King James word in Romans 6)? (p. 160) What does that mean for you on a daily basis concerning faith?


30.  Paraphrase Dan's words about being a brand new creature and being perfect.  What is he trying to tell us about our part in coming to know God's truth about us? (p. 160)


31.  What happens if we do not appropriate truth? (p. 160)


32. Discuss Dan's example about "Jesus acting like a baby in him." (p. 161) What do we need to do when this happens?


33. What does God say about our freedom of choice? Do you understand consequences and reaping what you sow? (p. 161)


34. What is our role for God to live through us and how does this work when we are feeling negatives? (p. 161-162)

## CHAPTER FIFTEEN—GOD'S PROCESS OF GROWTH

1. What is God's goal for us and what does He want our lives to express? (p. 163)

2. What are the three aspects of the first analogy/illustration that Dan uses for God's process of growth? (p 164, 1 John 2: 12-14) Upon what are these designations based?

3. What do the "little children" know? (p. 164)

4. What do the "young men" know? What is their emphasis? What excites them most? Who is their focus? (p. 164-165)

5. Is there anything wrong with being in either of these stages?

6. What do the "fathers" know? What are some characteristics of fathers? (p. 165-166)

7. How do we live in the father stage? (p. 166)

8. What is the second illustration of the process of growth? (p. 166) What are some characteristics of it?

9. Look at Dan's own testimony on pages 166, 167 and share an example from your own life where you acted out of the flesh. How did God convict you and how did you repair what you had done?

10. Where is the intensity of this battle taking place and what is God recapturing? (p. 167)

11. How can our process of growth compare to prisoners of war? (p. 167)

12. What is a person really saying who says, "My old habits and patterns are just the way I am and you can take it or leave it?" (p. 167) Do you have this attitude about any of your flesh patterns?

13. What will happen to a person's walk with God who has this kind of attitude?  (p. 167)

14. What is our part in the process of God recapturing the soul? (p. 168)

15. Who decides how and what circumstances will recapture our souls? (p. 168)

16. What three things does Dan say God can use to "force us back into the truth?" (p. 168-169)

17. What is the third illustration for the process of growth? (p. 169-170)

18. Which way does the body face?  Which way did God design the soul to face? What happened?  What is God working to do after one is a Christian? (p. 169-170)

19. In what areas does God want to woo back our souls? (p. 170) What are some of your areas that He is working on?

## CHAPTER SIXTEEN—SHALL NOT HUNGER

1.  What does Jesus say about us who have come to Him and believed in Him?  (p. 175)


2.  What does our soul tell us about ourselves? (p. 176)


3. Where do we look for the truth about ourselves, our hunger and thirst? (p.176)


4. What makes it important that we know that Jesus is our total sufficiency? (p. 176)


5. Do you know the river of living water or a trickle? Why or why not? (p. 177) What do you need to do if it is a trickle?


6. Which way does the river of living water flow after it has filled us first? (p. 177)


7. What is the truth about seeking first the kingdom of God?  Where is the kingdom? (p. 177)


8. What are some results of knowing we are finders and not seekers? (p. 177)


9. What are we to do when our old tapes play that say we are needy? (p. 178)


10. Why is it not helpful to keep seeking more of Jesus?  What can we say instead? (p. 178)


11.  Why did David get into trouble though he was a man after God's own heart?  (p. 178)


12. What methods and ideas does Satan use to trick us into believing his lies? (p. 178)


13. How did Dan process the pain of losing his wife? (p. 179)

14. How did Martha and Mary look at the problem of Lazarus's death? (p. 179)

15. Which place in "time" does Jesus want us to live? (p. 180)

16. What do we do with our wavering faith? (p. 180)

17. What brings us back to a sense of Christ's sufficiency? (p. 180)

18. What is ultimately the answer for all our needs? (p. 180)

19. What kind of peace is this Person to us when we hurt? (p. 181)

20. When we know that God is all sufficient what does our life look like? (p. 181)

## CHAPTER SEVENTEEN—THE HOLY BUT

1. How do we know that people always live after "the but?" (p. 183)

2. Where are we living when we put God stuff *before* the "but?" (p. 184)

3. What does Dan mean by "the Holy But?" (p. 184)

4. How did Jesus use the Holy But? (p. 184)

5. How is the Holy But a bridge? (p. 184)

6. Why is it important to admit the negative and say it first? (p. 184, 185)

7. What changes when we say God's truth *after* the Holy But? (p. 185)

8. How can our view of circumstances change when we know how to use the Holy But? (p. 186, 187)

9. Where does the shift happen as we say God's truth? What about the circumstances? (p. 186)

10. Why does it not really matter who is the origin of a situation? (p. 187)

11. Look at page 187 and contrast the differences in the soul and spirit. Where do we connect with Christ and draw our life? (p. 187, 188)

12. What happens when we doubt and blame others or God for our soul messes? (p. 188) Is there anyone in your life that you are blaming?

13. What healing and truth do you need to take to God in order to replace pain in your soul?

14. Look at Genesis 50:20 that Dan quotes on page 188. If you do not know the story of Joseph, read some of it and discuss how Joseph used the Holy But.

15. What is the comfort that you can tell to someone when they are in a fix that God fixed to fix them? (p. 189, 2 Corinthians 1:3, 4)

16. What is the battle that we have to go through to operate the Holy But? What happens when that is settled? How do you then go through the circumstance? (p. 189, Hebrews 4:11)

17. How does our victory influence ourselves and others? (p. 189)

19. Read Galatians 2:20 from page 190 and put your name in place of all the "I's." Say it aloud.

20. The world wants to see  truth before confirming. What is God's way? (p. 190)

21. What do we need to do in the process? What are some ways we can do this? (p. 190, 191)

22.  What is our permanent place of victory and rest? (p. 191)

## CHAPTER EIGHTEEN—TEMPTATION: A FAITH OPPORTUNITY

1.  What do we have to know before we will stop trying to fight the "swing?" (p. 192)

2.  Which aspect of the swing do most of us fight the most?  (p. 193)

3. Look at page 194 and discuss how Jesus dealt with His feelings about the Cross versus knowing God's will for His life.

4. Is temptation a sin?  Why or why not? (p. 195)

5.  Look at James 1:12. What is God's perspective of temptation?" (p. 195)

6. How do you know when you have gone from temptation to sinning?  (p. 195, 196)

7. How is a good way to make the commitment to refuse the temptation and go God's way? (p. 196)

8. How was Jesus (as human) able to do what the Father was asking of Him? (p. 197)

9. Describe some differences in the soul and spirit. (p. 197)

10. Did Jesus take any condemnation or guilt for his feeling in the Garden? (p. 197) What do you do when you have condemning thoughts?

11. Why does Dan say we are *meant* to be tempted? What difference does knowing this answer make in your life and view of temptation? (p. 197)

12. When does spiritual tension begin in a person's life? Why can we thank God for it? (p. 197, 198)

13. When and why would we need to pray, "Lead us not into temptation?" (p. 198)

14. What does one need to know in order to live victoriously? (p. 198)

15. Where does Satan have access to trouble us? (p. 198)

16. After we know union and the truth about temptation, how can we view Satan? (p. 199)

17. When will we stop having feelings and thoughts that bring temptation? (p. 199)

18. How do we learn to operate in our freedom? What can we do to help this grow? (p. 199, 200, Romans 7: 1-4) How do you know God's voice?

19. How are some ways that God teaches us in His schoolroom of life? (p. 200)

## CHAPTER NINETEEN—HEARING GOD

1.  Why is it important to know who is talking to you? (p. 201,202)

2. How can we know that we hear God's voice? (p. 202, 203)

3. How does obeying nudges help us learn God's voice? (p. 203)

4. Why does Dan say it is important to know the inner voice? (p. 203)

5. How can we know that the thoughts are not just "our own?" (p. 204)

6. What if results of following God's lead are not pleasant? (p. 204)

7. What if one doesn't hear correctly some times? (p. 204, 205)

8. How does Dan illustrate that the inner word is what is real? (p. 206)

9. What is the first practical point Dan makes about hearing God's voice? (p. 206, 207)

10. What is the second point? (p. 207)

11. What is the third point? (p. 207)

12. What will help us the most to manifest God through our spontaneous living? (p. 207)

## CHAPTER TWENTY—MAKING DECISIONS

1. How do the majority of people live life?  (p. 209)

2. What do we usually think when a decision produces disagreeable results? (p. 209)

3. What might be another way to look at disagreeable results? (p. 209)

4. How did Dan's experience with his first three churches teach him about understanding God's will? (pp. 210, 211)

5. What truth did Dan learn through these experiences after knowing union?  (p. 211, 212)

6. How was he living when he thought he was out of God's will at Church Two? (p. 212)

7. What was he using to decide if he was in God's will or not? (p. 212)

8.  Unless we so something heinously wrong, are we out of God's will?  Why or why not? How does this help you look differently at negative results?  (p. 212)

9. What does God do with our difficulties? (p. 212) What can you look back on in your life and see that God worked out in you instead of throwing you away?

10. How will we know for sure that we have sinned? How can we look at mistakes through God's eyes? (p.212)

11. What about times when we have to make a decision and don't have time "to pray about it?" (p. 212)

12. How did God show this principle to Dan by his question to some friends in 1989? (p. 212, 213)

13. What is our part after making a "quick decision?" (p. 213)

14. What is causing most Christians to get bogged down in trying to find God's will? What is the answer to that dilemma? (p. 213)

15. What can we do when feeling self doubt and fear about following God? (p. 214)

## CHAPTER TWENTY-ONE—DETACHED LIVING

1. What is one of the choices we have to make in order to truly experience Christ's abundant life? (p. 215)

2. How is union different from "another wedge of religious pie?" (p. 215, 216)

3. What needs to change in your life in order to concentrate more on what satisfies?

4. To what do we give our time? (p. 217) What is getting most of your time?

5. What generally makes people listen to Jesus gladly? (p. 217)

6. How did Jesus live a detached life? What does this mean to you and what changes might you have to make? (p. 217, 218)

7. What or whom are you holding onto and trying to get validity?

8. Look at the verses on page 218 about "quiet repose." What are different ways we can have quiet? How does one find inner quiet? (p. 218)

9. Why did the desert fathers run away to the desert? (p. 219)

10. What can happen when Christianity becomes easy? (p. 219)

11. What were the desert fathers really looking for? (p. 219) How can you find that without fleeing to the desert?

12. What are the conditions for knowing the Kingdom of God and having His best? (p. 220) What things are giving you a false identity?

## CHAPTER TWENTY-TWO—THE GIFT OF MISERY

1. What is this gift of misery? (p. 221, 222)

2. What did God teach Dan and Barbara through their gifts of misery? (p. 222) What has or is God showing you through your misery? What attributes of your flesh is he rooting out?

3. What did Joseph say to his brothers after his life of misery? How could he say this? (p. 222, Genesis 50:20)

4. Look at the story of Moses' life and misery on page 223. What did Moses have to learn before God could use him?

5. What did God say to Paul about human strength? (p. 224)

6. What are we to do with our gifts of misery? (p. 224)

7. Look at the story of David on pages 224, 225. What did David have to do with his sin? When did he do business with God?

8. Why do a lot of people come to conferences or for help? (p. 225)

9. When is God more likely to deal with us? (p. 225)

10. Look at the story of Peter on pages 226, 227. How did God bring Peter through his gifts of misery? What did Peter need to learn? What were the results?

11. Why does God keep sending our experiences until we learn the lessons? What are some of the things we need to learn? What are some results? (p. 228, Romans 8:28)

12. What current lessons are you in and what do you need to be honest with God about and lay at His feet?

## CHAPTER TWENTY-THREE—POURED OUT

1. How do most people believe that God loves? (p. 229)

2. What is *agape* love and how is it different than other kinds of love? (p. 229, 230)

3. Does *agape* love always feel like we think love should feel? (p. 230) Why or why not?

4. What are some characteristics of fleshly love? (p. 230)

5. Who chooses when and who we will love with *agape* love? (p. 230)

6. What do we do with selfish thoughts and feelings? (p. 230, 231)

7. For whom are we bearing fruit? (p. 231)

8. What do we need to understand in order to attract people to Christ? (p. 231, 232)

9. Who carries the burden of how we minister to others? What is our part in the process? (p. 232)

10.  When and where are we ambassadors for Christ? (p. 232, 233, 2 Corinthians 5:20)

11. What is God most interested in when He is ministering to others through us? (p. 233, 234)

12.  What is "true knowing?" (p. 234)

13. What does it mean to be "expendable?" (p. 234, 235)

14. What kind of lover is God through us? (p. 235)

15. What does it mean to be an intercessor?  How is this different from what most people think of as intercession? (p. 235, 236)

16. What is the cost of intercession? (p. 236)

17. What is the joy of intercession? (p 236, 237)

18. From which "stage" or level of the Christian journey do intercessors come? (p. 237) How can those in the child or young man stage be for others? What is the balance of receiving from Christ for our own needs and giving to others for theirs?

19. Are you focusing on how much God loves you? Is His love real to you on an experiential basis?

## CHAPTER TWENTY-FOUR—LOVING GOD

1. Look at Romans 5: 6-8 on page 241. List and discuss the various characteristics of God's love found on that page.

2. What is it that we want when we are in a temporary pit?

3. What did Dan tell his daughter might be a reason for us not sensing any strokes from God? (p. 241, 242)

4. What is the deeper level of knowing God? (p. 242)

5. Do you sense that God is closing a chapter in your life to begin a new one? What are some chapters He has closed and opened in the past? Are you learning to love Him for who He is and not what He does?

6. What does Dan suggest might be the main objective of God? (p. 243) How does this help us to *know* God?

7. In which stage of our journey do we love God in this way? What does it look like? (p. 243)

## CHAPTER TWENTY-FIVE—ENTERING GOD'S REST

1. What was Dan's misconception of rest before he found rest? (p. 246) What did it look like?

2. What does Hebrews 4:11 tell us about how we enter God's rest? What does this mean? (p. 247)

3. What is the key to entering God's rest? (p. 247)

4. What did Jesus say about rest in Matthew 11:28-30? (p. 247) What does that mean to you?

5. Where will we have the rest? (p. 247)

6. What does it take to rest from our own works as God did? (p. 247, 248, Hebrews 3:19-4:3)

7. How does Hebrews 4:12 (the heart diagram) fit in with this whole passage? (p. 248)

8. Where does the "diligence" or "labor of faith" come into finding rest? (p. 248, Hebrews 4:11)

9. What are some characteristics of finding God's rest? (p. 249)

10. How does God flow the living waters from us? (p. 249)

11. Look at page 250 and the verses about going inward. What are some results of finding the inner life with God? (p. 250)

12. What happens when we pursue the externals? (p. 251)

13. Where is the quiet place of rest? What is it like? (p. 251)

**Further Application:**

In a quiet place, assess with God or with the help of a close friend where you are in your knowing and experiential processes.

Are you taking the truth by faith? Are you asking God to show you through the Spirit? Are there any changes you need to make in order to help the processes?

Purpose to begin to "take" the truth by faith, because "what you take will take you."

# ANSWERS FOR THE QUESTIONS

**Preface**

1. [Personal answer]

2. Our life will be man-centered.  God will meet our needs, rescue us, we will be the center, God has to bless us.

3. With every spiritual blessing.

4. That we would be holy and blameless before Him, be His children.

5. For the praise of His glory.

6. That He might live and manifest Himself through us.

7. Everything comes from God, by means of Him and to Him are all things.

8. At the Cross

9. To manifest his life through us

## CHAPTER ONE—THE GATES

1. That life is supposed to be abundant and full.  There would be victory over sin and circumstances, rest, less struggling.

2. Salvation, our sins are forgiven. Appearances, works, goodness, money, religion. Underwear.

3. Personal

4. Sins are forgiven.

5. get tired of self-effort

6. Christ is with me to help me;  Personal

7. Feelings.  Personal

8. To give thanks in all things

9. Take off all externals. For him it was the charismatic movement.

10. Christ as the Life.  That He will live the Life.

11. He heard the truths and the Holy Spirit revealed them as truth. He already was righteous, holy, complete, loved, acceptable, and blameless.

12. That she was Dan's wife.  She had to give up that idol.

13. Gifts of misery

## CHAPTER TWO—THE LINE

1. A line. That God and truth are above the line, appearances and circumstances are below.

2. Above—truth, reality, God, rest, changeless, timeless, finished, unseen, eternal. Below—circumstances, appearances, striving, externals, seen, temporary, time, changes, need.

3. Above the line

4. He experienced all that we do or will, growth, temptation, needs. He has all power, knows the answers

5. We are perfect, complete, righteous, and blameless, beyond reproach.

6. We are to live by faith, we will know our true identity in Christ, we find fulfillment only above the line.

7. We will know God through faith; true satisfaction

8. A life of faith, true identity, fulfillment in life. Without revelation about them, we will live below the line.

9. How we understand by revelation from the Holy Spirit.

10. Revelation encounters our faith

11. What we believe. It doesn't matter what we say, what we believe will show up.

12. Sin will continue to have power over us, we will not be free and victorious.

13. Appearances, the seen and temporal.

14. That we and God are one, in union.

15. Promises become daily realities, no more separation, cease striving to get closer to God, we rest.

16. We operate by faith. Who we truly are. We rest. Our spirit. Personal

## CHAPTER THREE—DOUBLE CROSS, PART ONE

1. Christ died for our sins and external compliance with commandments.

2. Christ died for our sins.

3. Personal

4. How do I live this out? How do I get my act together? How do I keep from sinning?

5. We try to live the Christian life, we sin, we get forgiven, occupied with ourselves.

6. On ourselves. We are miserable, riding a roller coaster. We are seeing ourselves externally based on appearances.

7. Despair, condemnation, failure.

8. Sins are the product of something that dwelt in us before we received Christ—sin-- which is a power or force, rebellion against God, the source of sins.

9. A treadmill

10. When they go to Heaven.

11. Now

12. Knowing that he'd died and when I died.

13. He understood what it meant to be "in Christ".

14. Immersed into. Knowing I have been immersed into Christ means a world of difference about who I am, how God looks at me and how to live the Christian life. The diagram emphasizes that being in Adam or in Christ means "Whatever happened to Adam, happened to me, Whatever is true of Adam is true of me; then Whatever happened to Christ happened to me, Whatever is true of Christ is true of me.

15. Our old man, old nature, what we inherited from Adam that separates us from God. Dan uses the analogy of dandelions.

16. The human spirit indwelt by and enslaved to sin, expressing the desires of Satan. The Holy Spirit. Ephesians 2:1-6, Ezekiel 26:36. (For a visual of these truths, take a clear glass and fill it with water that either has soy sauce or coke or something in it that will make it dark. This is the old nature, a non Christian's spirit containing the spirit of error. As you describe the taking away of the old and replacing with a new spirit, etc, you will put away the dark liquid-- glass and all --and replace it with a new glass with clear water, showing the new spirit containing the Holy Spirit. You can say that most people believe that God adds some clear water to the dark, (that would be people who believe we still have the old nature) or that he pours out the dark and then puts in some clear. These don't quite do it, as it says all is new.

17. We will understand what is already true about us and stop trying to become something we already are.

18. The Blood side. Christ died for us. Our sins are forgiven.

19. The Body side. We are united with Him, participating with Him, old man crucified, new man risen with Him.

20. Blood is the juice/wine, Body is the bread.

21. It produces through us a quality of life that is unlike the world's; light in darkness, other love, victorious, changes our self image.

**CHAPTER FOUR—WHAT YOU DIED TO**

1. Her life would never be the same and she did not have to wait to die to be free and victorious.

2. Source of problems, sinful, enemy of God, separated from God, no real life, separation, death.

3. Receive it by faith

4. It shows us what it means to be "in Adam" and then "in Christ" and how being "in" someone means that whatever is true of them is true of us and whatever happened to them is happened to us. This is the basis for the whole truth of union. Look back at Dr. Solomon's diagram, #1.

5. That it means everyone but me.

6. We inflict punishment, guilt and condemnation on ourselves and try to get rid of the old and try to make the new come.

7. It is an accounting term that means count on it, know it is true, certain.

8. A creation is something made from nothing. A product is something made from something else. When we know we are a new creation, we can know that our past is not who we are, that we have a new life in our spirit. Though there are old patterns in our life and habits that need to change, they are not who we are.

9. He does not like them as they are not Biblical. What people mean by them is, I know that is true, but it is not my experience.

10. Take them by faith until we get the revelation from the Holy Spirit] [I bring out over and over any time Dan talks about getting to know these truths that we have to take them by faith until God does the revelation.

11. Sin and its power over us.

12. They are hearing through flesh and do not understand that when one knows he is in union with Christ, he will not want to sin.

13. When one understands union and that Christ is one's life, he will know that his true self wants to follow Christ and does not want to sin.

14. We sin because we are believing a lie at that moment, believing that we must meet our own needs, choosing to turn away from God and His truth. We live and walk out what we believe.

15. Our humanity or our environment, parents, schools were not. Sin was the problem and who we were. He became sin for us, removed the problem by us being crucified in Him, and replaced it with Himself.

16. In our spirit.

17. We can be pulled by the power of sin through our bodies and we can believe lies that are still trapping us spirit.

18. We feel the pull of temptation and think it is the real us. We then conclude that we are bad and have two natures.

19. It will show up externally as we learn to live from the truth of what has already happened in our spirit. We will live from the inside out and our behavior will slowly change to line up with what is inside as we believe it.

20. The law.

21. When the husband dies, the wife is free. It is us who died, not the husband. Christ is the new husband.

22. When the husband dies, the wife is free. It is us who died, not the husband. Christ is the new husband.

23. It keeps God from expressing His life in and through us. The lawgiver is now the law keeper in us.

24. Failure

25. Ourselves as as our point of reference.

26. If I do not know I died and think the old me is still alive, I am still my point of reference trying to correct me, trying to make something out of me. I am divided.

27. Sin, the law, myself as point of reference.

28. By continuing to say that these truths are not for me, about me; going by appearances and feelings. Tell God I want to know and to please reveal it to me and make it real in my life.

## CHAPTER FIVE—DOUBLECROSS, PART TWO

1. That God abides in him and he abides in God. Both verses say the same thing.

2. The new creation and that we are to live Life to the fullest.

3. So that God could unite Himself to our spirit and live His life through us.

4. The blood of the lamb died for the household. (Christ died for us) The body of the lamb provided life for them to get out of bondage (we take Christ into us for life).

5. [The lamb provided everything they needed. Taking it in provided the life they needed for their journey.

6. We will fail. It is impossible for us to do. The life is His and we have it when we have Him.

7. By His death and by His life.

8. Life without beginning or end.  Everlasting life has a beginning but no ending. Remember Dr.  Solomon's line, Diagram 1.

9.  Talking about no separation, that Jesus is living His life in me, through me, as me. Personal

10. Death.   We get results in our own efforts so they look like life. The difference is our motive and means for the results. Is it self-effort or is it God through us?

11. It often looks like it is us.  But it is Jesus living the life when we yield and co-operate with Him as He did with the Father.

12. No. Our true desire is to do the will of the Father.  We sin when we believe lies about life, ourselves, or God.

13. Who is the life?  Where is the life? Who am I?

14. Count on the truth, say the truth, and take the truth, trust Him, ask for the revelation, be willing and cooperate with Him.

15. Personal

## CHAPTER SIX—THE SWING

**1.** He began to have feelings for another woman, but realized his spirit did not want to follow through.

**2.** The last part about the thoughts and intention of the heart showed Dan the difference in his soul and his spirit because he knew the intentions of his heart were fixed towards God.

   (Laurie Hills' heart diagram which illustrates this verse can be found in my book Jewels for my Journey, where Laurie describes each part of this verse in detail.)

3. We go by our thoughts and feelings and think they are our real self.

4. The difference in soul and spirit and how to manage it.

5. He will keep telling us, "The old you isn't really dead. These thoughts and feelings are you. You are bad."

6. The eye is quiet, where the life and power are, and all the noise is out beyond the eye. The soul is turbulent; the spirit is fixed and unified. The soul is up and down, the spirit is where we are to live.

7. The top of the swing is our spirit, joined and anchored and secure. The bottom of the swing is the soul and body, seen and temporal, changes. We need to live from the spirit not the soul.

8. It is meant to swing. We don't like the fluctuations of thoughts and feelings. We try to stop the swing and make it stay on the "good" side of thoughts and feelings.

9. We think the good side is the "God side." But if the good is not originating above the line, from our union with God, it might not be God even if it looks good.

10. In the Garden, man decided that he would be the one to decide good and evil. So even if we are trying to do something good without God, it is still the wrong tree. Self effort is not God regardless of good results.

11. The focus is still ourselves.

12. Because God put it into motion and designed us this way.

13. That is the only way we can learn to live by faith out of who we really are and who He is rather than out of appearances.

14. We cannot crucify ourselves and it is already true that we died. We count on that as true until we know and experience it.

15. We will not take condemnation, our soul will not be a negative anymore, our focus will be on God.

16. We will see that He is always good no matter the circumstances.

17. The soul is loud and noisy; the spirit is quiet and still. We admit the noisy feelings and thoughts but live out of the quiet. We live in the midst of the noise, but from the spirit.

18. It knows what it knows by revelation. It is hard to explain in words. It does not know by analyzing.

19. Elijah began living from his feelings after a mountain top experience. He ran away and got depressed. He lived out his soul instead of his spirit.

20. If I believe that the noisy soul is the deepest thing in me, who I really am, I will live from the soul.

21. God was in it because He was there and managing the circumstances, but the wind, earthquake and fire (noise) are not where we find Him and relate to and follow Him.

22. He changes them into discipline or blessings, uses them for His glory, teaches us through them, and makes the truth real when we walk by faith.

23. In a still small voice, in our hearts/minds, in the quiet. We learn to know the difference between God's voice and Satan's and listen to God's by taking every thought captive.

24. I stand by faith on what God says is true and trust Him to live through me and show me in His time that it is true by revelation and experience. I do not live by appearances and feelings.


## CHAPTER SEVEN—ONE SPIRIT

1. By revelation from the Holy Spirit, not by probing, studying or analyzing.

2. Christ in you, He who is joined to the Lord is one spirit with Him.

3. There is an I and there is a He. We do not lose our identity, but neither is there a separation.  We function as one for God's purposes.

4. When we know and live out of our union with Christ.

5. We cannot get any closer than being one. There is no separation. He is not up there and us down here.

6. Personal

7. The tree of Life is a Person--Jesus.

8.  He looks like the uniqueness of each one of us, diverse and different, but still He.

9. Through having cancer, God showed Dan that he was right where God wanted him to be and that Dan was to live in the Spirit, not his soul or body. Cancer couldn't touch the real Dan.

10. Personal

11. Faith statements.

12. The male implants the life. The female manifests the life.

13. The husband's life.

14. Filthy rags. In the Hebrew this is the description of menstrual cloths.

15. Living by the flesh is the condition we are living in when we try to produce life, get our needs met outside of Christ, live by self-effort instead of Christ living through us, as us.  In the Greek, there are different words for "flesh" and for "old man."  The old man is our spirit indwelt by Satan before salvation. It died with Christ and is gone. The flesh can sometimes be referring to the body, but is also a condition that we can walk in when believing lies about life, God or ourselves. See Romans 8: 5-9 and note the uses of "according" and "in."

16. Because in the spiritual realm, we receive the life and manifest it like a female below the line when pregnant.

17. We do nothing except what Jesus does. We manifest His life. It will look like us.

18. No. It will be born.

19. I used to love hearing Dan say that when we know our union with Christ, that like the pregnant woman, the "baby" will come forth.  It assured me that some day, I really would manifest Christ's life.

20. Concentrate on God and His love in our union instead of how we have fouled up. By faith trust Him to live through us, as us.

## CHAPTER EIGHT—ONE NATURE

1. In the depths of our being we believe we are both good and bad.

2. If I believe this it will be impossible to live out my union with Christ and to rest. I will be focused on myself, on getting my act together, winning an inner war, and reject myself.

3. By understanding that the spirit realm, above the line, is singular and that what God says about me is true.

4. We will be controlled by whatever we believe is true and that is what we will live out of.

5. No, it is difficult because appearances and feelings make it seem true.  We stop focusing on feelings and appearances. We have to stop looking at behavior, appearances, performance, feelings, etc . to determine who we are.  We must separate personhood and behavior.

6. Two natures (children of wrath or partaker of divine nature); Two trees (Life or Knowledge of Good and Evil); Two masters (God or riches); Two fathers (God or Satan); Two Adams (Christ or Adam); Two slaves (sin or righteousness); two husbands (Christ or the law); Two vessels (wrath or mercy); Two spirits (Spirit of Error or Spirit of Truth); Two possibilities of behavior (good or evil).

7. We died to God and introduced the whole realm of duality below the line. (Dr. Solomon's line, Diagram1)

8. God and riches. We will love one and hate the other.

9. That neither of them was a Christian. The friend was and Dan was not.

10. Devil and God

11. They were judging by their own rules and interpretations as to what God would look like and do.

12. Who we are by birth , not by what we do.

13. Adam and Christ.

14. We are going by how we act, feel and think.

15. Sin and righteousness

16. We get mad at Him and think He is telling us to suppress part of our true selves.

17. The law and Christ

18. We commit adultery and we produce a nameless bastard--the filthy rags of self effort.

19. Wrath and mercy

20. Error and Truth

21. To whom do I belong? Whom do I confess?

22. We can do good or evil. We cannot be both in our true personhood.

23. It appears/looks true and we feel and think things that make it seem so. We look at and take by faith what God says about us and who He says we are.

24. What I do does not have anything to do with who I am. Behavior and personhood are different.

25. Misery. We can do what we want or not do what we don't want to do. We can't walk consistently. There is endless self effort. We are doing all the work to look good.

26. Birth, not performance determines our identity.]    [If you bark like a dog, are you a dog?]

## CHAPTER NINE—THE REAL YOU

1.  We get attention from behavior, we get approval or punishment from behavior, we get liked or disliked from behavior.

2. Personal

3. To use the struggle for acceptance and love to create the self in us that wants to try to get along independently of God.

4. The body and soul operating apart from the Holy Spirit.  Immorality, impurity, sensuality, idolatry, sorcery, strife and good things that did not originate with God.

5. When we operate from self-effort even good things like self-reliance, self-discipline, religious activity, good deeds are of the flesh.

6. What and how we are used to operating, the false self. Manipulating the false self to be more effective; living in self-reliance and independence. The damage from either lacks of necessary things or traumas that were bad needs to be healed by Jesus. These old wounds cause patterns of believing that affect our present life.  Jesus wants to renew our minds by replacing those lies with His truth. Personal.

7. Ourselves

8. Personal

9. We look at ourselves and others through God's eyes and not through humanity. Our emphasis is on Christ.

10. I am a new creation, I have a new spirit, a new heart, I am born again, I am raised up and seated with Christ in the heavenlies, I am righteous and holy. [Remember the object lesson with the dark water.]

11. A creation is something made out of nothing. A product is something made from something else.

12. We live out of what we believe. What we deeply believe, not what we say, will determine our behavior.

13. We will live from whatever we say after the but ] .[There will be a whole chapter later on the Holy But.

14. Personal. [The answer is no.]

15. When he stopped trying to become who he wanted to be and saw that he already was.

16. Make a list from the book.

17. Mature. There is emotional maturity, spiritual maturity, physical maturity, social maturity. A person can know lots of Scripture and be very immature emotionally and relationally. Healing is needed for childhood damage and lacks. Life skills are needed for relationships. Below the line, maturity is done in community. People need to grow in all different ways.

18. Knowing our true identity gives us a deep awareness that there is not any condemnation.

19. Satan's voice condemns and lies. It is performance based. God's convicts, points out, corrects. Satan's is loud, selfish, causes fear and doubt. God's is quiet, loving and accepting. God's encourages faith, unconditional love, and truth. They can both be heard as thoughts in 1st person singular, especially Satan's to try to trick us into thinking it is us with that bad thought.

20. It enables us to live with a Christ-consciousness instead of a sin-consciousness.

21. We know from God in our spirit, not by condemnation or false guilt]

22. We confess our sins, receive the forgiveness that is already there and thank Him that we are forgiven. 1 John 1:9, confess means agree with.

23. We are saints not sinners after salvation. Look at how Paul begins most of his Epistles to "the Saints." Note that the Corinthians' behavior was not good and he still called them saints.

24. Thank Him and rejoice that we are forgiven.

25. We are living with ourselves as our point of reference, not acknowledging who we are and who Christ is in us. It is not real life. It is fake—a false self.

26. Anything or anyone that is giving me my identity. When we are not using externals to get our needs met or get our identity. Personal answer.

27. The answer is not more effort. When God reveals Himself to us, we see the things freely given to use. We simply receive by faith. When we know union, we will actually sin less. We will live out of not wanting to sin and not trying to get needs met the wrong ways.

28. It is my personal opinion that "me and God can work it out" is not the only way to grow and deal with issues. I do believe that knowing union is most of the battle, but I also see the need for various ways to grow and get healing through counseling and community.

29. I am not a sinner, but a saint. I am God's holy, righteous, blameless child. I have his nature and I desire to do His will.

30. We accept/receive and take it by faith against the appearances and feelings. We receive it and ask Him to make it real in experience. A little formula to show this: **Truth + Faith + Holy Spirit = Experience**

## CHAPTER TEN—GOD'S PRECIOUS ASSESTS

1. A thing of value.

2. Being obliged in law, responsible, answerable.

3. I will feel inadequate, that I do not measure up and want to get my act together.

4. He will use it somehow in our life or in somebody else's or both.

5. He wants to express Himself through us and he uses our soul and body, thoughts and feelings.

6. The radio waves are out there in the air but cannot be expressed without the radio. The spirit is there but has no point of contact without us and our humanity.

7. All parts of us. Personal answer.

8. We contain Christ but we are not He. We cannot produce His life.

9. Trying to produce the life, be the contents or do things in my own strength would be like chewing on a Styrofoam cup instead of drinking the coffee or Coke.

[At the bottom of page 113 it seems to me that it is okay to have someone appreciate us and notice that we are a Christian if in our heart we know it is God and He gets the glory and that it is not necessary to say it is God to the one noticing. Our motive for taking praise would be the key.]

10. A reflector that shows what is there. It tells the truth. We are a reflection of God's essence, the means of His essence. We reflect His glory. Personal

11. We are receivers and expressers.

12. Unnatural

13. There is no striving and He lives His life through us. It is not frustrating but easy.

14. There are not a lot of changes in our basic personality. But there is a process of learning new truth that renews our minds. God grows and matures us and modifies things in our personality that do not operate according to His ways. We are to accept ourselves and others as we are and until He does His work, and leave the timing to Him as well. Some traits are neutral and won't change. I believe that the bottom line of what He changes is what we are believing , which, when the lies are fixed, brings about outward changes. Our spirit does change and our behavior changes as we become more aware of who we are in Him.

15. When we are open and vulnerable about our warts and blemishes, our humanity and the lessons that God has or is teaching us.

16. We can praise and thank Him for them, realizing God will use them in other's lives.

17. We need to get help to find out why and how to stop harmful habits. It will work better in the changes if we rely on God and His strength and not do this in our own strength.

18. Personal

19. We need to get help to find out why and how to stop harmful habits. It will work better in the changes if we rely on God and His strength and not do this in our own strength

20. By knowing that his outer humanity is God's perfect instrument and how He touches the world.

## CHAPTER ELEVEN—REVELATION: GOD'S WAY OF KNOWING

1. Intellectual is just information in the brain/head and we try to grasp God's truths without the Holy Spirit. Spiritual is from the Holy Spirit and is known in our heart. Intellectual knows about, spiritual knows.

2. The frustration brings us to the end of self-effort. God means us to be frustrated and does not want to interrupt it before we are completely frustrated in order to prevent us thinking we made it on our own.

3. They force us to ask the right questions.

4. "Why did God let this happen to me?" "How can I fix this situation?" Flesh answers tell us we have to earn something or there is something wrong with us. They tell us we have to do something outside of our union. Look at p. 125 where Dan talks about 'know about 'means earn and 'know' means freely given.

5. A good spirit question would be, "What is God trying to show me, teach me in this situation?" "What do you want to do here, Lord?" Spirit answers are present tense and

involve something that is freely given. This discussion is vital and goes along with the Single Eye which is the next chapter.

6. When we get desperate and reach the end of all flesh questions.

7. The answer is a Person, Christ Himself.

8. From God to our spirit where the union is.

9. Know about means we must earn something, know means it is freely given and to be received.

10. We live from separation instead of union; God is up there and I'm down here. I have to try with God's help.

11. I am established in that truth.

12. That I have been crucified with Christ and it no longer I who live, but Christ lives in me. If you do not know that your sins are forgiven, get with a friend or pastor who can help you know.

13. It is not hoping, feeling or thinking. It is important because when we don't know the difference, knowing seems based on feelings and thoughts. But it isn't. In knowing, you and knowing are one. You become mixed or united with the thing you know.

14. By revelation and experience. The revelation can be instant and direct without teaching and is not intellectual. Experiential happens as what we know becomes mixed with us and is real in our life.

15. God uses circumstances, situations and trials. If we get the revelation first then during a trial, circumstance, etc. we will have to say the truth that we had the revelation on. If we have not had a revelation on some information we have, then we have to say the truth about it during the circumstance in order to get the revelation. Either way we have to take/say the truth.

16. The Biblical word "know" indicates union. It is not intellectual, but experiential. Cookie dough, coffee with sugar and cream, chlorine in a swimming pool.

17. By taking it until it takes us and we become in experience what we took and took by faith.]

18. I am forever changed. I can't go back. It is very hard to sin in an area where I've had a revelation.   In our spirit.

19. He teaches us with tailor made lessons based on our individual situations.  He uses our life experiences and circumstances. Our awareness of Him grows.  It is God's good pleasure and timing that decides.

20. He glorifies and declares the Father and Christ. He is the means by which Christ's life comes forth through us. He is the teacher, guide and comforter.

21. We agree with and cooperate with Him.

22. There is no condemnation, There is no separation, You cause all things to work together for good]

23. We always live out of what we <u>know.</u>

24. The noise and chaos of the seen and temporal, our circumstances.

## CHAPTER TWELVE—THE SINGLE EYE

1. Dan had to use his nest egg to pay for surgery. Personal answer.

2. He chose to see what God was doing instead of seeing only external appearances.

3. Because it is truth and if we don't we will experience and reap only the external situation, missing God and His blessing.

4. He uses a specific incident to get me to focus on so I will stop and look at what He wants me to look at.

5. The Single Eye.

6. Personal

7. He doesn't look at who caused it but at what we will do with it, how we will take it into ourselves. There is a place for Spiritual warfare, but it is not to be our focus as the enemy is already defeated.

8. By how it looks and feels, whether they consider it good or bad.

9. God is sovereign and all is part of God's domain and He will use all our circumstances. He means it for good.

10. This is where the witness takes place. He ministers through us and wants us to see as He sees and know as He knows. We learn to live by faith.

11. He is saying that God uses even evil to accomplish His purposes. God is in everything and means it, but all is not God. The devil is defeated and God takes his tricks and lies and turns them around on the devil.

12. See them as someone or something who God was willing to sacrifice for our growth. We can thank God for them.    Personal

13. He could go into his soul and cry and grieve and go back to his spirit and say the truth with God in the union.

14. They become an oasis for other people.  This is where they receive the life. Personal

15. We can remember the past times that God met us in the desert or tell each other about our times there with Him.

16. They are for other people.

## CHAPTER THIRTEEN—THE RULE OF GRACE

1. We do, by trying to keep God's law.

2. That Christ was in them and would live through them.

3. Jewish Christians who believed that the Gentile Christians had to be circumcised and keep all the Jewish laws.

4. Peter was fellowshipping with the Gentile converts until some Jewish Christians came from Jerusalem and he would not fellowship with them anymore. Paul rebuked Peter.

5. No. We have to choose. If you try to keep any of the law, you have to keep all of it all the time.

6. We will find out that it is impossible and we will fail. We will live under condemnation and "death" until we know we are free from the law and can't keep it in our own effort.

7. Our flesh or false self. The flesh wants to try and wants God to help instead of trusting Him to live through us.

8. No, It is holy and good and has the purpose of bringing us to Christ.

9. Futility, frustration and failure. Personal.

10. To bring us to the end of our own resources and trying to get our love and acceptance outside of Christ so we will know that Life is found in Him and Him living through us as us.

11. Again, we separate behavior and personhood. Failing does not make one a failure. Some people are high achievers and fear failing and thus fight coming to the end of themselves. Others see themselves only as failures, living in defeat and depression. Both need to know that they have died to themselves as the point of reference.

12. The death with Christ included death to the law. I am free from the law and Christ lives in me. The Lawgiver is now the law keeper in my heart.

13. It was made with God, Jesus and Abraham. It was based on faith not law.

14. There is no life in the law. See 2 Corinthians 3:6.

15. It would always be the death knell for the complete gospel of Christ in you the hope of glory.

16. It is not common to find people walking free from the law and others can think you are a heretic. They can't "see" Jesus as you.

17. Because we never get away from the temptation to go back into it.  Performance based acceptance is everywhere and engrained in us.

18. Personal

19. Go ahead and have at it. Do it your way and I will be here when you come back.

20. They are opposites – grace is absurd in appearance but life giving,  law is sensible in appearance but death bringing. Once we get out from under the law, we will not go back very easily.

21. Because I will not be easily driven back to it.

22. Walk in the Spirit and you will not fulfill the lusts of the flesh. Most churches/Christians walk or believe like this verse is reversed in its order, (Don't fulfill the lusts of the flesh and then you will walk in the Spirit) which results in living under the law and self effort.

23. Behavior, self-effort, performance, co-dependency, non-acceptance, not seeing things or people through God's eyes.

## CHAPTER FOURTEEN—WHO DOES WHAT?

 1. It is exhausting and does not work. It is like a roller coaster, dealing with the false self and below the line.

2.  God initiated it, God fulfills it, God will complete it. It is all on God.

3. We believe that we have to fill up whatever is missing, that living the life is on our backs.

4. We are to know that we are already holy in our inner being and trust God to bring that into our experience and behavior. It is all His work. We agree and co-operate.

5. God is doing all the work to make me new. Remember the illustration with the dark water? He also does all the work of causing me to walk in His ways.

6. We no longer have a relationship to the law or have to try to fulfill it. God will manifest His character through us. He will keep the law in us.

7. [As He is living His life through me, it will look like me to others, but I won't be the person it began with or who it is. The life is His.

8. Make a new covenant, put my law in their heart, be their God, all will know me, forgive their sins, remember their sin no more.   Give you a new heart, put a new spirit within you, remove the heart of stone, give you a heart of flesh, put my Spirit within you. Personal

9. Personal

10. We try to make it happen in our own efforts.

11. A new heart, new spirit within us, removed old heart, His Spirit in us.

12. He will cause me to walk in His statutes. He is making my outer behavior match what is true inside. He is doing it in His ways and timing.

13. To be willing <u>and</u> co-operate.

14. The lie of independent self and self sufficiency. If successful, you get more self, vainer. If not, you get self-condemnation.

15. Personal

16. To live His life of doing the will of the Father through us. The Holy Spirit is in us as the Teacher, to line us up with the true Person in us.

17. The more understanding of His nature that He gives us, the more our behavior lines up with who He is and who we are. It works from the inside out.

18. Degree by degree, from one degree of glory to another.

19. He doesn't know Christ lives in Him to do the living. He lives out of his soul (feelings and appearances); he operates as if life originates with him.

20. Until one knows how to operate out of their true identity and union, they need specifics. When someone first becomes a Christian they might not know much about God's ways so they might need some guidelines as to what the Bible says. But this is not done with condemnation or performance based acceptance.

21. His goal was to present everyone complete in Christ by knowing that Christ lives His life through them, as them.

22. When one begins to live from the reality of Christ in them and learns to allow Christ to live through them.  We will sin less as a result because we will understand we don't want to sin and Christ will fulfill the commands through us.

23. We will quit trying to be good, we will be free from pretending, we will stop being religious.

24. They are trying to do something external to become acceptable to God, themselves and others.

25.  I am already dead.  I will try to get rid of something that God wants to use for His glory and what He wants to use to press me in to Him and get me to walk by faith.

26. We are to be willing and not try to do God's part. We do this by faith and trust, not self effort.

27. I obey by believing. I believe that I died with Christ the same way I believed that He died for me.  Colossians 2:6.

28. We don't try to die. We recall the fact and live it out by faith. Hebrews tells us it can be a labor to enter because we have to go against strong soulical feelings and appearances.

29. Reckon is a banking term that means you can count on having the money. Counting on the fact. This is what we do everyday concerning being dead to sin and alive to God and the union we have.

30. I am a new creation and I am perfect because God says it is so. I don't look it or feel it all the time or act it, but it is true. I have to come to a place to agree with Him about it in order to experience it and be free.

31. We are caught in a flesh trap forever. We will ride the roller coaster of feelings and live below the line. We will be miserable and fail trying to keep the law.

32. Dan's behavior did not look very mature, but He acknowledged that God was still there. We need to admit/confess/agree with God that our behavior stinks and then thank Him we are forgiven and go on. If others are involved, we need to seek their forgiveness if we have offended or hurt them.

33. He gave us complete freedom of choice but if we go the way of the world or try to go our own way, we will reap the consequences of those choices. Personal

34. Our role is availability so He can live through us. We trust Him to do it. When feeling negatives acknowledge that we cannot do it and trust that He will as we make ourselves available and allow Him to do it through us.

## CHAPTER FIFTEEN—GOD'S PROCESS OF GROWTH

1. To take us from external to internal; for us to live from the union and not the soul or body. He wants us to express in everyday life what is already true about us.

2. Child, Young man, Father. They are based on one's level of inner knowing, not on chronological age.

3. That their sins are forgiven and they have a relationship with the Father.

4. That they are strong, they know the word of God abides in them, they have overcome the evil one. Their emphasis is on themselves. Power, excitement and adventure are what excite them.

5. No.

6. They know God. They know Person, they have entered into the union with that Person. They are settled in and calm, they are understanding, sympathetic and compassionate towards others.

7. We live by faith, not sight, in the fellowship of His sufferings, we experience the union and our life is for others. See Philippians 3:10

8. Recapturing the soul as manifestor of God. We are like a windowpane with God shining forth with some distortions from fingerprints (flesh patterns.) He wants to work on those old patterns.

9. Personal

10. It is in our soul. God is retaking the territory that was stolen from Him so that He can manifest Himself by means of us. It is a slow process.

11. The soul has been freed from captivity, but it has old habits and patterns that are engrained and sometimes we fear walking out into our freedom.

12. This attitude comes from fear of pain, fear of facing the past that made these old patterns and unwillingness to yield to God and His process.  Personal

13. God will never capture one inch of his soul.

14. We are responders to Him. We hear and obey and allow Him to take our soul in love.

15. God alone.

16. The storms in our soul, the world system and its ways, the pain and turmoil of feelings.

17. A visual of the body, soul and spirit.

18. Body faces outward. Soul designed to face the spirit. He is wooing our soul back from the outer to the inner, turning it slowly back to Him.

19. Every area where our soul is turned outward. Personal

## CHAPTER SIXTEEN—SHALL NOT HUNGER

1. We shall never hunger and never thirst.  NEVER.

2. I am hungry, thirsty, needy, just hanging on.

3. If we look below the line, we will believe we are hungry and thirsty. If we look above the line we will see the Truth.

4.  Besides helping us live in victory, it affects how we are able to be light for others. We can give without worrying about lack.

5. Personal

6. Away from me to others.

7. We are finders not seekers because we already have the Kingdom within us.

8. Freedom, no longer anxious about ourselves and our state, know we are full, not trying to get life from other people or things.

9. Remind ourselves and each other that Jesus is our total sufficiency.

10. We already have all of Him and He can't give us anymore of Himself. We can ask for more awareness of Him.

11. He was listening to the lie that he had a need that God was not meeting.

12. He raises the question about God's sufficiency and often uses the word "if." He provides noise and distractions to try to get us to supply that need ourselves.

13. He rejoiced in his spirit, took God as his sufficiency and felt the pain of the sadness in his soul.

14. They focused on the past and the future.

15. In the present, in the now. He is the I AM.

16. We ask Jesus to help our unbelief. We focus on the truth of His presence and His sufficiency.

17. Realizing that He is present and in control.

18. The answer is a Person—Christ.

19. He is Peace which passes all understanding.

20. Circumstances are not quite so critical, we don't have any spiritual needs, we don't hunger and thirst, we have the Life, and we are satisfied. We feel feelings but don't live there.

## CHAPTER SEVENTEEN—THE HOLY BUT

1. It is evident in their lives that no matter what they say, they live by what comes after the but.

2. In the junk, in the circumstance, below the line.

3. We say the God stuff after the but and it is a bridge that moves us from the stuff we are in to faith and living by faith.

4. In the Garden, He voiced His pain and feelings and then said, "But Thy will be done."

5. It moves us from the soul level to the spirit level and to faith.

6. The negative is real and often painful and difficult, so we admit it and then say the Holy But.

7. There is a shift on the inside and where we are living from changes. We can't change the stuff, but we can change how we are going to receive it and view it.

8. They no longer control us and pull us down. We see Jesus in the circumstances as the solution. We go from external to internal.

9. The shift happens inside us. The circumstances may not change at all.

10. Because when we use the Holy But we turn to God either way and look to Him as our source and life and solution.

11. The spirit is unchained and free, Satan is off limits, there is perfect harmony with Holy Spirit, it is at rest and quiet, running smoothly, where life is. The soul is seldom in harmony; it is pulled and tugged with strife, high and low.

12. We won't get free of anything nor have peace until we somehow take things back to God for His answer and healing.  Personal

13. Personal

14. Although his brothers meant for him to die, Joseph saw that God had worked in all of it to bring them to the point where Joseph would save all of them and the people of Israel.

15. How God brought me through something similar. How He is sufficient, in control, loves us; not to deny the pain.

16. The battle is to go against the intense feelings and old beliefs and walk in faith that is most likely opposite. It is settled when it is won.  I can then go through it in God with victory.

17. We look different than the world and it is a witness for others.

18. Agreeing with God and putting what He says after the but.

19. Personal

20. Say what is true and then He will confirm it.

21. Repeat it often. Say it out loud when you can. Catch the thoughts that are lies and not true. 2 Corinthians 10:4. Say the truth to others, have others say the truth to you.

22. We see what God sees. We say what God says. We live as He lives through us.

## CHAPTER EIGHTEEN—TEMPTATION: A Faith Opportunity

1.  That God put it into operation as a prerequisite for faith choices.

2. Temptation

3.  He felt His intense soul feelings and accepted that they were okay to feel and not a sin. He voiced what He wished could happen. Then He said, "But Thy will be done."

4. No. We can think about or feel things without acting on them.

5. We are blessed to persevere under it. God doesn't tempt us. We are tempted when carried away and enticed by lust. What is lust?

6. When lust is joined to the act, then it gives birth to sin.  When we join ourselves to it, which can be just knowing or saying to ourselves that "given the chance I will do this" even if we hadn't actually done it yet. This is what Jesus meant by committing adultery in the heart.

7. We say the temptation (thought or feeling) first then say the Holy but with God's truth after.

8. In union with God, with the Father, doing it through Him.

9. Soul makes noise, inner turbulence, disturbs us, humanity gets pulled and tugged with feelings and thoughts. Spirit is the realm of knowing, quiet, we just know, God is the point of origin for life.

10. No. He knew it was God's natural process to move Him to faith. Personal.

11. Temptation is the means to take us to faith. Without it there would be no such thing as faith. Personal

12. When we become a Christian and are born again. We thank Him because it is proof we are alive to the Spirit.

13. When we do not really know yet that we died with Christ, after first saved.

14. We have to know that we are dead to sin.

15. Below the line, in the soul and body.

16. We can see that he is not really an enemy in the sense that he is under God's control. He is defeated already. He no longer has any power over us.

17. After we die physically.

18. We learn to hear the Spirit of God inside, know His voice and follow Him. Personal

19. He woos us back to Him in the different places in our lives. He wants us to know His sufficiency and rest in Him. He does the lessons again and again until we get it. Then when we know, we know.

## CHAPTER NINETEEN—HEARING GOD

1. It will affect your choices and how you walk out life.

2. He says if we are His we do. We know in our spirit.

3. We will find out slowly but surely what His voice sounds like to us individually. It will be a sign of our faith. He will continue to move us along.

4. Because God has set it up this way to be an inner kingdom where He is joined with us and wants to live through us. He does it most fully when we hear his voice and obey it.

5. Because we do not have a desire to hear any other voice. It's by faith. We decide we've heard from Him.

6. We do not decide based on results. We just trust Him with the result and continue on without condemnation.

7. Do not focus on the failures. Don't worry as you learn to listen, eventually you will learn. Trust and listen to Him the way He talks to you. (Going by Scripture does come into this discussion and we want a balance of being careful not to claim to hear God saying things that would not be like Him to say or that go against His word. Also, there are times that He says to do things that seem crazy to onlookers, but He will not lead against His character.)

8. God told him he was free from cancer. God did not tell Barbara she would be healed.

9. We will most often hear His voice in the mess, when circumstances and soul are in turmoil with negative feelings. His voice will be quiet and sometimes won't come until we get still.

10. We can spend time with Him alone, just listening.

11. We will do what God wants us to do. Even when we lived in self-effort, we were trying to do what God wants. Our inner man is always in agreement with God.

12. The more we know Him and hear Him, the more we will manifest Him through spontaneous living.

## CHAPTER TWENTY—MAKING DECISIONS

1. 99% spontaneously.

2. That we sinned, missed the mark, or made a mistake.

3. That we have made a mistake might not be true.

4. That he did not make a mistake by taking any of them. God was working out what He wanted to happen with Dan. He never was out of God's will.

5. That God is in everything. He was never out of God's will.

6. He was living out of appearances.

7. The way it felt and the results.

8. No. God uses all of it and just works it again. Personal

9. He uses everything in our lives and works everything to our good. Romans 8:28. Personal

10. The Holy Spirit will tell us. There really aren't any mistakes and He uses all our decisions.

11. We believe even in our haste that He is present, He is the guidance.

12. He simply asked the friends a question that got him a job that provided insurance for his wife's illness.

13. Trust that God is making it through us and don't worry or watch the consequences. Just watch for Him.

14. Living from a sense of separation. Knowing that there is no separation, We are one, He lives in us, through us and guides us.

15. Say by faith that my self is out of the way. I do not want to decide to do evil or make selfish decisions.

## CHAPTER TWENTY-ONE—DETACHED LIVING

1. We have to choose to detach ourselves from a preoccupation with the values of the world.

2. Union is a new lifestyle so dramatic that we might have to reorient our lives.

3. Personal

4. To whatever is our passion. Personal

5. When they don't have any appearances to live on.

6. He was detached from the world not looking to anything external to enhance His identity. There was nothing He wanted to possess more than the Father. Personal

7. Personal

8. Minding our own business, less stress, be alone, go on a retreat, inner peace. Inner peace is first a Person who lives in us. The more we trust Him and live in our union the more we will experience inner peace.

9. Christianity had become a state religion which turned it into an external thing.

10. When there is no sacrifice or persecution, it becomes too easy. It is a religion that is external.

11. They wanted to develop their spirit oneness with God. They pursued Him internally. We can do that now because we know life is in the union and we are living an internal life with Him.

12. Detaching from everything and anything that could give us a false identity. God wants to give us the reality of the Kingdom. His gifts are freely given. Personal

## CHAPTER TWENTY-TWO—THE GIFT OF MISERY

1. A gift from God that involves circumstances that contain pain, heartache, disappointment, discouragement, but brings us to Him.

2. He taught Barbara not to have Dan as her god. He humbled Dan from legalism, pride and self-righteousness when Dan had feelings for another woman. Personal. Personal

3. "You meant evil against me, but God meant it for good." God used his misery to mature him and to bring temporal salvation to his father's household. He chose to see the purpose of God in spite of the appearances.

4. That he could not rely on his own accomplishments, his human power or self effort. He thought he didn't need God.

5. "When you are at your weakest, I can be My strength in you."

6. Thank God for them. In the misery is our strength, our hope, our everything, our life.

7. No excuses, he was honest, he uncovered his hidden sin. He did this at his lowest point, when his life was falling apart.

8. They hope that God will get them out of a fix, but they have to come to see He is in it and decide if they want Him or to just get out of the fix.

9. When we don't have anything else to bargain with, nothing left but our filthy rags.

10. Jesus prayed that his faith would not fail after he denied Jesus. Then Jesus restored Peter with His three questions after Peter repented. He needed to learn not to have his confidence in himself but in Jesus.

11. He wants us to learn of Him rather than excusing and denying. We signed on and gave Him rights and privileges to do what He pleases. To be honest, to thank Him for our gifts of misery, to use the Holy But. We will have a new life, strength in Him; we'll be a disciple who is not above his master. We will know Him.

12. Personal

## CHAPTER TWENTY-THREE—POURED OUT

1. Most think He loves the way people do.

2. It is not natural to fallen humanity; it is not based on performance or feelings. It acts for what is best for the other person, not sentimental sympathy. It can be tough. There is not preoccupation with self and one is lost in what God is doing for the other person.

3. No. Sometimes it can feel tough, but it contains what is best from God's perspective.

4. One is a taker, the love is not satisfying; it is selfish.

5. God

6. Take them to God and admit them then say the truth that we are for others and He will live through us as us.

7. For others.

8. That Christ lives in me, I am the light of the world and the salt of the earth, His love expression to the world.

9. God decides and uses us where we are. Our part is to be available and cooperate, trusting Him to live through us.

10. Everywhere that is my world, whether work or play.

11. He is most interested in what is best for the other person, not me. He puts specific people in my path.

12. When God brings us to the place where we have ceased from any activity that has it beginning point with us. We know we are experiencing Him in our inner being and He is quiet in us. We are no longer striving to get needs met outside of Him.

13. Expendable means "used up." Just like Jesus, I may have been able to rescue someone else but now will not be able to save myself. He will want to live His life through me in humbling ways that may not be earth-shaking.

14. He doesn't need rewards, applause, acclaim, but loves for the sake of loving.

15. An intercessor is someone who bears the sufferings of Jesus, who is willing to stand in that place, be the light in the darkness, take the rebuff, be sacrificed so other will come to the Father. Most people think it is just praying.

16. Laying down one's life. It is not necessarily physical death. We are fools for Christ, without worldly honor.

17. We give our life for others. We get to see others know who they are, come to know Christ, and learn to walk in victory.

18. Intercessors come from the father stage. Those in the child and young man stage can serve and help as they are able, but their focus will be more self-oriented. Everyone can give somewhere. None of us can give without receiving first. We must be like a conduit from the Spirit filling us for the living water to go out to others.

19. Personal

**CHAPTER TWENTY-FOUR—LOVING GOD**

1. Christ died for us when we did not deserve it. He didn't get anything back, no reward. He just loves even if no one ever loved Him back. He is love. He cannot do anything else.

2. Stroking and rewards.

3. Some of the pain you feel when you don't get any strokes is part of the process whereby the real love the He has poured out in your heart comes out. He is loving Himself with His own love through you.

4. He might take away something like outer rescues and strokes that were satisfactory in the past in order to replace them with something better—knowing Him deeper.

5. Personal

6. That we just love Him.  When we fall in love with Him, we will know Him deeper and vice versa.

7. This is the father stage.  It is the most spirit and soul-satisfying experience possible. It defies description.

## CHAPTER TWENTY-FIVE—ENTERING GOD'S REST

1.  He thought it was just a kind of passive existence. He wanted to get away from the regular routine and shift into neutral.

2. We have to be diligent [labor] to enter it. This means that we may have to go against feelings and appearances that say it is not possible. For some, it may take healing from lacks or traumas in childhood that taught them not to be able to rest inside.

3. We cease from our own self-efforts and enter by faith. It is not ceasing from all activity.

4. Come to Him and He will give rest. Learn of Him and His yoke is easy and light.

5. We will find rest in our soul.  Peace will be inner, lined up with our spirit where the union is.

6. Quit trying, believe the truth and follow Him.

7. It is in the context of rest. We can't enter God's rest as long as we are living on soul based appearances and feelings instead of by God's Spirit.

8. The labor or diligence can be from how hard it is to say the truth against feelings and thoughts and appearances. Sometimes we need help from another person to even do this. It is not the same as trying, but it can feel like difficult labor to go against the feelings and appearances.

9. We breathe a sigh of relief. We say, "I'm home."  I am back with the Father. The rivers of living water flow.

10. When we mind the journey inward.

11. I live with the Father, I know Him, and outer things fade and drop away. I have a new identity, I am truly liberated and free, I am content in whatever circumstances.

12. They become idols to us, we will worship them and we will miss the life.

13. It is in God, not in this world, not in senses, not in the soul. It is an inner rest from striving.  It is real.

Printed in Great Britain
by Amazon

33531229R00046